To our dearest Ralegade

Thanx for all your wisdom & Love

Marci ♡ ☆

Thank you for so much Aunty Winnie. Greatest Love Prit

MARGARET ROBERTS' ANIMAL PRAYERS

Published by Spearhead
An imprint of New Africa Books (Pty) Ltd.
99 Garfield Road
Claremont 7700
South Africa

(021) 674-4136
info@newafricabooks.co.za

Copyright in published edition © Spearhead 2003
Copyright in text © Margaret Roberts

All rights reserved. No part of this publication may be reproduced or transmitted in any form or by any means without prior written permission from the copyright holder.

First edition, first impression 2003

ISBN 0-86486-557-0

Layout and design by Jenny Wheeldon
Illustrations by Mike Thayer
Cover design and artwork by Mike Thayer
Photograph by Phyllis Green
Origination by House of Colours
Printing and binding by ABC Press, Cape Town

Acknowledgements

I am absolutely thrilled that Spearhead's publishing manager, Jeremy Boraine, has taken this little book and made it happen. He stood reading the prayers in the chapel and said he felt there was a place for a book like this, even in the precarious publishing world of today, where such an unusual little book would be engulfed and lost forever, or never have even started out on its life journey. How heartened I am that so many have urged me on, so many have wept over the prayers, and so many are ready to donate their hard-earned cash to the animals.

All proceeds from this little book will go to animals in distress, all over our country.

I thank the typesetter for giving her time and expertise to the book and to the many tireless workers behind the scenes – I am so aware of your hard work and energy that you give unstintingly.

To the fundraisers and the organisers who put together events to urge the public to part with their money, may this little book lift a little of your load and smooth a small distance of your way, and may it continue to do so for many years to come.

My gratitude goes to my long-time friend, Jeanette Horn, the most talented "scribe" I know – for her design and layout of the prayers on the chapel walls.

And to Mike Thayer, one of South Africa's most brilliant young artists, for his exquisite drawings. How wonderful it has been to, at last, put together a book with him like this.

To animal lovers, and to the animal welfare workers, and to the dedicated teams of loving ladies who brave the abattoirs and who stand in prayer as the animals go through the rush pens to their deaths – they know, they hear your prayers and it makes their last journey perhaps a little easier.

This little book is for you all, a great heartfelt salute to each one of you. Keep on keeping on, you make the difference. Maybe the slaughter and the killing will one day cease.

May God be with you all.

Contents

Introduction v
The Prayer of All Creatures Great and Small 1
The Prayer of the Ant 2
The Prayer of the Little Bee 4
The Prayer of the Beetle 6
The Prayer of the Butterfly 8
The Prayer of the Cat 10
The Prayer of the Caterpillar 12
The Prayer of the Chameleon 14
The Prayer of the Chicken 16
The Prayer of the Crab 18
The Prayer of the Cricket 20
The Prayer of the Dog 22
The Prayer of the Dolphin 24
The Prayer of the Donkey 26
The Prayer of the Dragonfly 28
The Prayer of the Ducks 30
The Prayer of the Flea 32
The Prayer of the Fly 34
The Prayer of the Flying Ant 36
The Prayer of the Frog 38
The Prayer of the Glow-worm 40
The Prayer of the Goat 42
The Prayer of the Goldfish 44
The Prayer of the Grasshopper 46
The Prayer of the Guinea-fowl 48

The Prayer of the Hedgehog 50
The Prayer of the Homing Pigeon 52
The Prayer of the Horse 54
The Prayer of the Ladybird 56
The Prayer of the Lizard 58
The Prayer of the Millipede 60
The Prayer of the Mole 62
The Prayer of the Monkey 64
The Prayer of the Mosquito 66
The Prayer of the Mouse 68
The Prayer of the Ox 70
The Prayer of the Owl 72
The Prayer of the Parrot 74
The Prayer of the Peacock 76
The Prayer of the Pig 78
The Prayer of the Praying Mantis 80
The Prayer of the Rabbit 82
The Prayer of the Seagull 84
The Prayer of the Sheep 86
The Prayer of the Snail 88
The Prayer of the Spider 90
The Prayer of the Squirrel 92
The Prayer of the Starfish 94
The Prayer of the Swallow 96
The Prayer of the Tortoise 98
The Prayer of the Very Little Bird 100

Introduction

Ever since I can remember, each night on my knees I would add a long list of pleas to my prayers for 'those who cannot speak for themselves', as my grandmother put it. Pleas for their protection on a stormy night, pleas that the animals should not be caged or whipped or isolated or abandoned, pleas that all mankind should love and nurture the animals and the birds and the fish, and to stop the killing.

I wept, and still do, helplessly, over the throw-away animals – those pets that are tossed out of cars, left to wander in terror on busy roads, and I weep ever more at man's lack of caring and inhuman behaviour, and all heaven weeps too.

I cannot count the lost dogs and cats that would come to our farm gates with such desolation in their eyes in their never-ending search for their owners – those who had thrown them away. With every passing car their eyes and their hearts lifted in that desperate hope that their heartless owners would come to fetch them – only to have each hope dashed.

My grandmother taught me to pray for animals when I was about seven years old. On a never to be forgotten day, while walking down a dusty road, we witnessed an old horse being badly thrashed. She stopped, and still holding my hand, said a prayer out loud asking for God's protection for the horse, and a kind heart for the angry man who held the whip. In a few minutes the man stopped and walked away. The horse pushed open the gate, limped over the road, came and stood before us, and lowered his head in front of my grandmother. She continued her prayer, telling the horse God's love surrounded him, while she stroked his lowered head. I have never forgotten that moment, as I knew without doubt, the horse had understood and had heard her prayer. From that day I started saying prayers for animals, birds, insects and even fish out loud.

We had a colourful and somewhat terrifying teacher, a Miss Goedhals, at Brooklyn Primary School in Pretoria, where I spent a safe and happy childhood. Miss Goedhals had scraped back black hair, bright red nails and lips and a bad-tempered Maltese poodle forever on her arm. She was formidable, and if we were at all naughty we would be kept after school to write out, not lines, as most of the other teachers did, but the prayer for animals. It was my Standard II school friend Martin Reitz who, on reading the prayers on the chapel wall at my Herbal Centre, reminded me that it was Miss Goedhals who made me write out my first prayer for animals, which sowed the seed for the animal prayers. Martin sent me the original poem, which is reproduced on the following page:

A Prayer for Animals.

Hear our humble prayer, O God, for our friends the animals, especially for animals who are suffering, for all that are overworked and underfed and cruelly treated, for all wistfull creatures in captivity that beat against their bars, for any that are hunted, or lost, or deserted, or frightened, or hungry, for all that are in pain or dying, for all that must be put to death. We entreat for them all your mercy and pity, for those who deal with them we ask a heart of compassion, and gentle hands and kindly words. Make ourselves to be true friends of animals and so to share the blessings of the merciful.
Amen

AUTHOR UNKNOWN

During my matric year at Pretoria Girls' High my favourite teacher, Mademoiselle Verdier, who taught us French, gave me a book on which to practise translation, *Prièrs dans l'Arche* – 'Prayers of the Ark' – by Carmen Bernos de Gasztold, who lived at the Benedictine Abbey at Limon-par-Igny in France. This book was so utterly charming that she let me keep it because I could not put it down – I was so overcome that someone else was praying for animals. Several years later, I built a cottage on the farm for Mademoiselle Verdier to come and spend the holidays with us. To this day I can see her sitting on the long benches under the trees on hot summer afternoons, or cosily in the big armchair in front of the winter evening fire, and hear her soft voice reading the prayers both in French and English to my children. And so the prayers became interwoven in our hearts and minds and became a part of us all.

Many years later I built a new little chapel in the Herbal Centre gardens – a small place for peaceful prayer and contemplation, a non-denominational place of quiet with a plaque outside it welcoming visitors into its cool, music-filled space:

> *Welcome friend from anywhere*
> *Never mind the clothes you wear*
> *God looks on the inner heart*
> *Pray in peace, in love depart.*

My daughter, Sandra, made the exquisite stained glass windows and together we chose beautiful and uplifting prayers to go onto the walls. I wanted to put some of Carmen Bernos' prayers onto the rear wall, but it was Sandra who urged me to write my own prayers so that we could then perhaps raise much needed funds with the prayers for animals in distress.

And that is how I began to write the prayers, with gratitude to my grandmother who showed me that a beaten horse heard her prayer; to the late Mademoiselle Verdier who made me translate *Prièrs dans l'Arche* and later read the prayers to us all, over and over, during the holidays, and to Sandra who makes things happen with all her love, support and care for all lost and injured animals, and who has to be one of St. Francis' most loved assistants.

I couldn't ignore the homing pigeon club's Gert Mulder, who specially asked me to write the prayer of the homing pigeon, which has now gone out to pigeon fanciers all over the world. I couldn't ignore the two deep sea fishermen who read every prayer on the chapel walls and who asked me to write the prayer of the dolphin – I wrote two, at different times, and they chose them both. I couldn't ignore the old lady from the Kalahari who wept so heartrendingly over the donkey's prayer as her own donkey that pulled her cart for twenty years had died recently. She understood the donkey's prayer so well.

And, I couldn't ignore the many visitors who begged me, so sincerely, to put the prayers into a book so they could be read and re-read again and again. And this is how it came to be.

But then, amidst all the uncaring in this frenzied world of ours, there are those who do care, who love their animals deeply and who rely on them for companionship in sickness, loneliness or old age. In my own anguish and grief which I have known so intimately over the years with so many beloved pets, I have had to go beyond my own loss, and never more so than when my companion of 17 years and little lifesaver, Spik, became so desperately ill that nothing could save him.

I had to watch my dog linger in his last days, refusing to eat no matter how I tempted him. I am sure he stayed to comfort me, to help me through because I had become so ill with pneumonia. When it was finally thrust upon me, I had no choice – the decision had to be made in haste. It was my doctor, who, having gone through this same heartache, gave me this beautiful poem. I in turn gave it to my vet, who gives it to others who are going through the final decision in the dark days. Whoever the anonymous poet was, there will always be a great number of people who are and will be, so grateful for it.

If it should be

If it should be that I grow frail and weak
and pain should keep me from my sleep,
then you must do what must be done,
for this, the last battle, cannot be won.

You will be sad – I understand.
Don't let your grief then stay your hand.
For this day, more than all the rest,
your love and friendship stand the test.

We've had so many happy years,
what is to come can hold no fears.
You'd not want to suffer so,
when it's time – please let me go.

Take me where my needs they'll tend,
only stay with me until the end,
And hold me firm and speak to me,
until my eyes no longer see.

I know in time you too will see,
it's a kindness that you do to me.
Although my tail its last has moved,
from pain and suffering I've been saved.

Do not grieve that it should be you
who must decide this thing to do.
We've been so close – we two these years –
don't let your heart hold any tears.

Living on a farm with children's pets, beloved dogs and cats, horses, bantams, chickens, ducks and even a precious house-trained muscovy duck called 'Sweetie', we all learned early on to have a little burial ceremony and to put flowers on small or large graves, but nothing diminishes the aching, except time.

And it is because of all of this that this little book came about. It is extraordinary how the pieces slot in and the pages find their way to completion. I have been writing the prayers of the animals for a long time. Now it is time to share them with you.

So here they are, for each one of you. Fifty prayers and the first one I wrote 'The Prayer of All Creatures Great and Small', spoken by all the animals and insects and birds and fish that are around us, written for our hearts and our thoughts and for our ears and our eyes, so that we can be their true friends, and help them and so 'share the blessings of the merciful'.

May the prayers spread love for the animals and caring for our world and stir us each to fight 'for those who cannot speak for themselves'. May they make a difference.

Herbal Centre
De Wildt
Northwest Province
South Africa
Summer of 2003

The Prayer of All Creatures Great and Small

Dear Lord,
Hear our chorus of thanksgiving
for the beauty and glory of Your earth,
for Your trees, Your plants, Your rivers, Your seas, Your mountains,
Your winds, Your sun, moon and stars
and all else in the wonderland
that You have given us each one.
From the tiniest ant to the greatest king elephant,
our voices are in harmony, in praise and thankfulness.
We revere and respect this magnificent world,
but we watch in helplessness, while man, with all his brilliance and
cleverness, yet gives the earth its saddest sound, daily
destroying and polluting Your beauty.
So many of us, Your unspeaking creatures, are becoming extinct
because of man's greed and thoughtlessness.
Is there no way to send a shaft of light into his stony heart?
To awaken his spirit, to awaken love and caring and humility?
To help him see the consequences of his uncaring?
His greed? His thoughtlessness?
In dumbness we too are praying for all mankind.
Oh! let them hear our pleas. Watch over us, Lord.
Our very existence is threatened.
Amen.

The Prayer of the Ant

Oh Lord!
I am this speck, this minute dot, yet I live!
Am I not a tiny miracle?
Am I not a force to be reckoned with?

I am trampled, unnoticed, I am squashed under their great feet.
Yet I survive – am I not a true survivor, Lord?

In this little scrap of life You have created,
You gave me the heart of the lion, the strength
of the elephant and the cunning and brains
of all Your creatures put together!

Thank You, Lord, for my greatness!

Everyone knows a little ant cannot move a tree, a house,
a bridge, a road – yet, with the skills, the diligence,
the cleverness, the persistence, the endurance, the pure sheer
never-giving-upness You have bestowed me, I can,
in the dirt and darkness, undermine everything – oops,
there goes another rubber tree, oops, there goes
another bridge – You see …

Just help me, Lord, to be more into building up than into breaking down, with my cleverness I can bring in the armies, and move mountains, and change the face of so much.

Help me to build up, Lord.

Help me to teach them, Lord.

And let them marvel at me, one of Your tiniest creations.

Thank You, Lord.

Amen.

The Prayer of the Little Bee

Such dedication, such diligence,
such buzz-buzz busy-ness
You have given me, dear Lord.
There is so much to do – Your days aren't long enough.

Such a wonderland of scents and sights
You put before me – drenched in nectar and sweetness.
Thank You, Lord, for the beauty of Your flowers and their
kaleidoscope of shapes and colours. I never tire of them.

Weren't the flowers Your most loving, happy creation?
I like to think so, and as for creating them for me,
dear Lord, my tiny heart bursts with love and pride.

I'll make honey for You, Lord, for the world!
I'll do anything for You, Lord.
You have given me skills such as no other creature.

See how neatly I built those exquisite combs,
how cleanly I work,
how lovingly I nurture our lazy queen,
how I mother the little lives she lays,
and how I work, Lord,
to exalt You and the wonder of Your world.

I'll give them honey, Lord, to sweeten their lives for You, Lord.

Is heaven also filled with flowers? I think so!

Thank You. Thank You.

Amen.

The Prayer of the Beetle

Dear Lord,
Am I not Your little soldier – armour-plated
and tapping out a message for You to hear – tok-tok-tok?
It means look and listen and give thanks, thanks, thanks.
Are they looking and listening and saying
thanks, thanks, thanks, Lord?

Thanks for the rain.
Thanks for the lovely rotting vegetable matter.
Thanks that we are so adaptable.
Thanks that we can survive the desert, the drought and heat.
Thanks that our shiny armour shells can condense the dew.

Tok-tok-tok. Thanks, thanks, thanks, Lord.
Is this called Morse code, Lord?
Do they still tap out messages
or have they forgotten how to say thanks?
We know we are little symbols of luck, Lord,
busy tapping out our message of gratitude.

Would You tell them how any three good words
tapped out together can make waves all around the world?
Make them look at us, Lord, and listen and learn.
Here they think we're calling a mate only – yes –
we are – but we're also sending You our loving, Lord.
Let them try the loving too.

What about peace, peace, peace?
Tok-tok-tok. Love, love, love?
Tok-tok-tok. Joy, joy, joy? Tok-tok-tok.
There is no end, Lord. Rain, rain, rain.
Light and love and health and caring.
What a world, Lord!

Tok-tok-tok.
Thanks, thanks, thanks!

Amen.

The Prayer of the Butterfly

Oh Lord!
This beauty! These flowers! My little fragile life is far too short!

I don't really like being a caterpillar.
I get eaten so quickly by those greedy birds –
could You not hasten my wing growth?
I would so love to fly to You, Lord,
and alight on Your hand to say thank You,
face to face, for Your flowers.

I know You painted flowers on my wings.
Am I not a floating, fluttering flower
freed of rooted steadiness?
I tell them it is so lovely to feel
the wind beneath my wings,
to view them from above like You do, Lord.

Even if it is only a few exquisite days
that I can exalt in Your sunlight,
Your early morning dew, Your scents,
Your nectar, Your flowers – especially the lavender –
I can, like happiness, alight on the shoulder
of a worry-laden human when they're not looking,
to lift their spirits by my pure pretty presence.

I can touch them with a tiny blessing from You, Lord.

*I can be Your little light carrier, just for a moment,
even if they just look at me and marvel at my painted wings –
how beautifully You paint, Lord.*

*Thank You that You gave me my brief moment in Your sun,
that I can stir a cold human heart for a second or two,
that my little lightness of being lifts a little of the darkness.*

Give me strength to fly to You, Lord, where I belong.

Amen.

The Prayer of the Cat

Dear Lord,
I am so self-sufficient, haughtily asking little of
anyone, asking little of life, except a safe warm spot in the
sun, a curse on the whole race of dogs, a daily bowl of
milk and sardines, and a patch of clean loose sand,
a warm bed I can snooze on when it suits me, and a
doting human or two who stroke me so lovingly.

Thank You for giving me a busyness of thought
and singular and independent ways for making
me superior, and quite undemanding, and for giving
me that aloof self-sufficiency most of the time.

I do my bit, Lord, to keep Your world a better
place, like catching those sinister rats and stupid
mice, who spoil so much.

Help me to remain agile and quick in reaction
and decision, and to keep my nine lives intact.

*Thank You for my suppleness of limb, my quickness
of eye, and my softness of night-time step.*

*I purr my gratitude to You, for the pleasures of that
patch of catmint which I relish, and for Your sun, and for
Your birds who never cease to fascinate me.*

There is so much to watch in Your great world, Lord.

Thank You.

Amen.

The Prayer of the Caterpillar

Dear Father,
We marvel at Your ingenuity to give us such stages in life!
So fast – just when we think we have it all worked out;
we change into something else!

We seem to be continuously bursting out!
But we do know the best is yet to be!

It is in this stage, Lord, that we are at our most vulnerable.

It is now that we are hunted down by, not only Your
voracious birds, but by that crushing boot when they
discover we've eaten away their lilies and their other plants.

Don't they know You created those luscious leaves for us, Lord?

We really are insatiable at this stage – we don't even lift
our heads to observe the dangers of our brief life.
It's just chomp, chomp, chomp and on to the next leaf.

How quickly we can turn the toughest leaf
into a delicate lacy skeleton!

Why does it infuriate them so?
Do they not know we need to eat to give our butterfly wings
strength when we bind ourselves into that stifling cocoon?

Do they not understand that from this fat and bulging
worm-body with its tiny tippy-toes, a breathtaking
beauty will emerge soon? A beauty so fragile in its
fancy-winged flight they will marvel at us?

Protect us from the squashing, Lord. We can't wait
to fly to You, Lord. Give us patience, but hurry Lord!

Amen.

The Prayer of the Chameleon

Dear Lord,
I know I am one of Your strangest creatures, a small relic
from the age of the dinosaurs, from a forgotten time,
my measured, swaying steps so thoughtfully executed.
But, Lord, am I forgotten too?

Am I merely a curiosity, waiting in my slow, swivel-eyed
cautiousness to be crushed and stoned, to be roughly,
carelessly, hurtfully handled with shrieks of laughter?

Are my extraordinary colour-changing abilities a mere game?
Am I to be thrust onto hot tarmac to change to grey, onto
searing red tiles to change to red, onto burning tin roofs
to change to blue or black or green? Why, Lord?

Can I not just merge into the softness
and kindness of nature, Lord?
Do my beautiful mottled colours
not do justice to true camouflage?

Oh, hide me Lord, I who walk with careful steps,
my fear showing in my constant slow-moving vigilance.

*I cannot rest, Lord, my heart pounds in apprehension as
I strive to hide from human hurtfulness.*

*I try to zap those annoying flies, those blood-sucking
mosquitoes, to make the world a better place, on my
elastically extended tongue.*

But, am I just a curiosity, Lord?

*Oh! make them marvel at my uniqueness, in my
two-toed lonely progress, and hide me, Lord, please hide me.
My survival is so questionable.*

Amen.

The Prayer of the Chicken

Dear Lord,
It is so hard to be eaten!

It is so wearisome to be continually laying all these eggs!

I feel so comical with my clucking and pecking, but what else is there to do? No-one takes me seriously!

I am such a loving mother, darting about, watching over my chicks, clucking and caring.
Some humans could take a few tips from me.

Your love beats in my feeble chicken heart.

I am not brave, not clever, but when my chicks are in danger I am dauntless. That is because You love me the way I love them.
But save us from the hawks, oh Lord!

Thank You Lord. It is enough that You love me.
It does not matter that no-one else does.

But do You think You could save me every now and then from the Sunday roast, or from their favourite chicken soup?

*Yet Lord, if it can nourish and help someone feel better and restore health to the sick, then I have not lived in vain.
For which I say Amen.*

*But don't You forget me, Lord – and thank You
for all those seeds You give me to scratch in.
I'm so busy looking after my chicks, I almost forgot!*

Amen.

The Prayer of the Crab

Dear Loving Father,

What a strange creature I am. Hard and resilient outside, with a strong armour of protection. Yet, so soft and jelly-like an inside that is all a quiver of fright and flight.

I am incessantly nervous. Could You calm that frenzied scuttling, and give me a little time to rest? A little moment to find myself? I am quite breathless, Lord, with all this watching and waiting! Do my eyes have to be permanently out on stalks?

Is it because I am just so constantly scared?

Comfort me, dear Lord, tell me loudly that, in the safety of Your hands, I have nothing to fear – for You are with me.

Poised on my little tippy-toes I hardly touch Your earth, I find shelter in Your rocks and crevices. Oh, hide me, Lord! I seem to scuttle hither and thither, a frenzy and a terror beating within me.

Does all that frenzy show I am lacking in faith?
The faith that says 'Let go and let God'?

Why these claws, Lord? They give such a wrong impression.
Are they there to ward off trouble,
clicking weaponry in action?
If so, Lord, let me be Your little soldier,
give me a brave heart and steady the jelly inside.

Are You behind me, Lord?

Amen.

The Prayer of the Cricket

Dear Loving Father,

Is it only You who love us?

Did You have to make us so chirpingly noisy, Lord?

Does all this clever chirping have to infuriate them so?

We silence the bow string of our rasping, while they search for us to quieten the night's cacophony, that ever-ready torch and boot ready to crush out their anger.

We know we rob them of their sleep, Lord, but how is it that the nicest, safest, driest places always happen to be under their bedroom windows?

What is our purpose, Lord, other than penetratingly tearing the quiet night-time peace?

We have such busy scuttling night lives, Lord, we patrol Your ants' nests and have a taste for so wide a variety of things. We don't think we're a nuisance, Lord, and we love to hide in tight nooks and crannies, defying their search.

We climb, we hop, we crawl, we burrow, we squeeze,
and boy, can we scuttle!

Should we feel a little sorry that we have such
a loud and irritating presence, Lord?
We really are rather clever, Lord – thank You for that.

You must have had fun giving us these resonators and no
voice, but such an ingenious sound system. No-one
believes we can do it with our strong legs, Lord.

Thank You, Lord, for making our presence heard,
for whatever it is worth!

Amen.

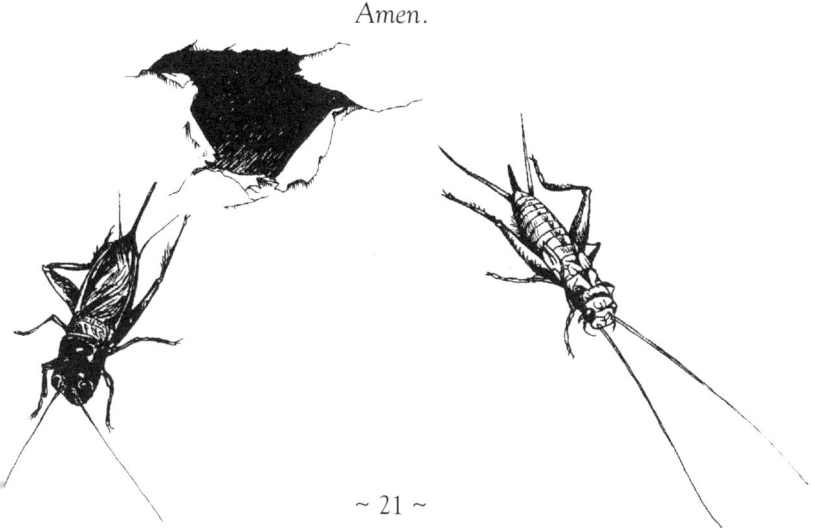

The Prayer of the Dog

Dear Lord,

Of all Your creatures it is I who love You most, Lord.

*I am overcome with devotion and unconditional
love for my human masters. Unquestioningly,
unrestrainedly and completely, I pour my love out to them.
I could die for them, Lord.*

*I ask so little of them, Lord – just the occasional
pat, the occasional stroking of my coat, the occasional
kind word, and a walk, oh please!*

*I hear it and see it all, Lord. I am at their side, I will
follow them to the ends of the earth, and it breaks my heart.*

*I will protect them. I forgive them over, and over, and over
like You do, Lord.*

*I will not sleep while they sleep – I will guard them,
watch over them, as You do Lord.*

*But when they leave me Lord, when they lock me up and
go away – can they not feel the desolation within me?*

*When they close me in tiny spaces where I cannot
run, cannot see out, do they not hear my pounding
desperation, my panic rising, never to be stilled?*

*When they forget that life-giving bowl of water,
when they forget to feed me, what of their sharp kicks,
their whips, their lashings? Oh Lord, strike compassion
into their hearts – let them ache a little when they throw
me out of the car at the side of the road.*

*Let them feel a little pain when they abandon me
when I am old – I, who am so filled with love I could die.
Oh let me die Lord, and come to You
to feel Your love, Lord.*

Are You hurting too, Lord?

Amen.

The Prayer of the Dolphin

Our Father who art in heaven, is not some of Your heaven here in the blueness of the seas? That is, where it is not thick and dank with human waste?

What of these humans Lord? Do they know we are here to help them as we have been since You first created them?

Can they not hear us, Lord?

Can they not think, Lord?

Why do they pollute the preciousness of the greatest thing on this planet – the sea?

Why do they cast nets and kill us and hunt our brothers, the whales, and the tunas and the shad and the barracudas? Why, Lord, do they do it for fun, Lord? Do they love the hunting and the spearing and the ocean red with the blood of our dying anguish?

And those terrible terrifying nets, Lord? Have they no heart, Lord? Can they not think, Lord?

Can You show us a way to reach them,
Lord, for their own sake?

Please, Lord, give us the sounds that will take away
their need to kill, to dominate.
Give us the abilities to show them our knowledge
and vision of Your greatness, Lord.

We weep with You, Lord. Their wars, their greed,
their driven killing destruction of all that is beautiful,
but we strive, Lord, from our salty depths to help them, with You.

Oh! Surround us with Your protection, Your safe harbour, Lord.

When will they ever learn?

We wait Lord.
Amen.

The Prayer of the Donkey

Dear Lord,
I am heavy in heart, in step, in spirit, in loneliness.

I trudge wearily with my load, downtrodden,
poor and lost, so lost.

I am thrashed, beaten, tied and neglected.
Meagreness surrounds me.
They have forgotten that one exalted day long,
long ago, on Palm Sunday, I carried Your Son.
His cross is marked on my back,
evermore to remind mankind of my role –
the most precious load I ever bore.

They have forgotten.

Please Lord, set a star to watch over me, I am so alone.

Help me to know that one day I will again walk with Your Son.

Help me to forgive.

*Help me to find a safe, quiet field, a few weeds to eat,
and set my heavy heart and voice still while I wait for You,
away from the uneasiness and stress
of the harsh world that engulfs me.*

I am so beaten, so longing for kindness.

Speak louder Lord, the days are too long … I am too alone.

Oh! Take me home, Lord.

Amen.

The Prayer of the Dragonfly

Oh Lord,

I flit in this frenzy of fastness over Your precious spreads of water! Oh Lord, this wonder of water!

Even in my silky cocoon I could hear it, smell it, feel it. Is there any more precious substance on earth, more wondrous, more life-giving, than water?

I reflect that beauty in my fragile exquisite wings, in the iridescent hues of my lean, light body – I exalt over the surface-shine, darting here, hovering there, checking it all out for You, Lord.

Surely it is I who is Your most dedicated water-watcher, Lord? Bursting with gratitude that I can witness the water lilies' opening buds, the darting of the little fish and hear the song of the frogs under the stars.
It is such a paradise Lord, this water world!

Help me to make them aware, Lord, these humans who pollute, destroy, drain and desecrate Your lifesaving ponds and rivers.

Make them notice, Lord, let them see me, let them hear my silent voice of reverence for Your water, Lord, quickly, before it is too late!

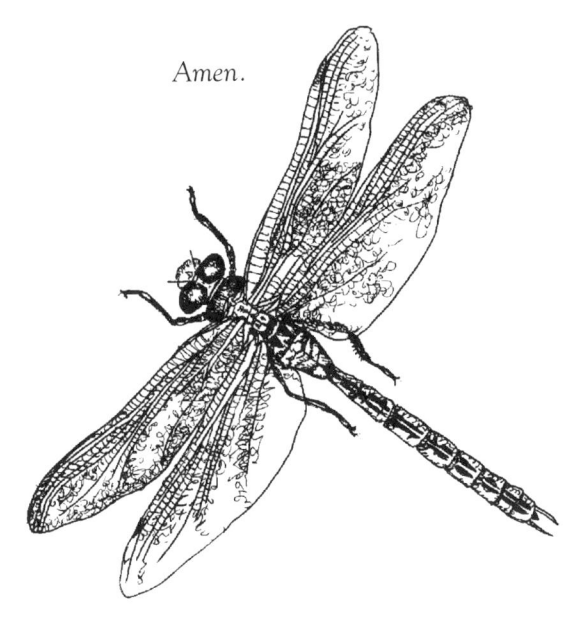

Amen.

The Prayer of the Ducks

Dear Lord,

*Bless every pond and pool, puddle and river,
stream and vlei and lake.*

*Let it rain every day, now and forever, for with the rain
comes the lushness and the lusciousness of water plants,
of delicious little slugs and snails, and a green and
inviting world that teems with life and thankfulness.
Can You hear the pulsating thankfulness?*

*Not only does the life-giving rain beautify our world,
but are others aware it is the lifeblood of our very existence?
Are they aware of the extreme preciousness of every drop?*

Do they revel in it?

Do they treasure it?

Do they guard their water?

Are they waterwise?

Make them aware Lord, those unthinking humans,
the way You made us aware.
Thank You for our webbed feet, Lord,
that propel us so swiftly through Your blessed water,
and even for our quacking monologue.

Can You hear us saying 'thank You, thank You'?

Protect us from our many predators and make those
unthinking humans lose their taste for duck casserole.

If so, we should say 'Bless You, Lord' and 'Amen'!

The Prayer of the Flea

Dear Lord,

*I must say, for all this little speck of life that I am,
I have the power to drive both man and beast wild!*

*What a talent, Lord! I hop, I skip, I flit, I wriggle, I bite,
I hide, I spring, I crawl, exasperating them all!*

Am I a vicious little beastie, Lord?

*Am I delighting in their ineffective and furious slappings
and scratchings too much, Lord?*

*I hop, I skip, I flit, I spring. And what discomfort I can bring!
It just shows You, Lord, that being small is powerful!*

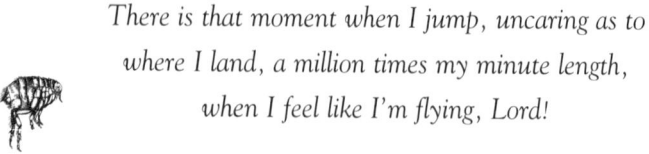

*There is that moment when I jump, uncaring as to
where I land, a million times my minute length,
when I feel like I'm flying, Lord!*

*Is that why I leap onto the dogs and the other animals and
the birds and those striding humans, hide in their hair and burrow
into their feathers, just to catch a ride of high jinks?*

*I explode into laughter as it takes only a second
to get them into a frenzy of scratching!*

Oh Lord, am I wicked and naughty and selfish and useless?

*I worry a little at their infected fleabites that I leave as I nip
and bite, but not enough to stop my nipping and skipping.
It's such fun, Lord! Can You hear my laughter?*

*I hop, I skip, I flit, I spring.
What discomfort I can bring! Sorry Lord!*

Amen.

The Prayer of the Fly

Oh Lord,

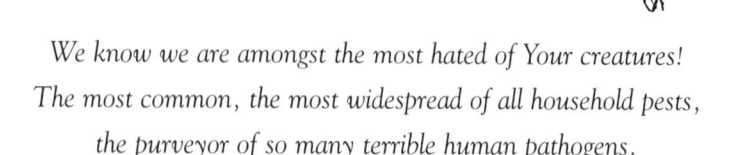

We know we are amongst the most hated of Your creatures!
The most common, the most widespread of all household pests,
the purveyor of so many terrible human pathogens.

How is it that we, in our tinyness, can spread so many appalling
diseases, like cholera, dysentery, typhoid, anthrax, leprosy,
parasitic worms, infections, hepatitis, to name but a few?

No wonder we are so detested.

Our dirty, sticky little feet love to trample the cesspool,
the foul drain, we search out all manner of putrefying
flesh and disgusting excrement, our ever-hungry proposces
searching out every foul and filthy speck which we buzzingly,
busily deposit upon their food, all over their kitchens – we love
kitchens – and even upon them themselves and upon
their pets who we can drive to a frenzy!

Is there hope for us, Lord? What are we to You, Lord?

Should You not swat us to death the way they do, Lord?

Would it not be better to close our bulging crops that store so much germ-laden filth that we regurgitate and deposit so deftly on their food?

Would it not be better to be squashed and beaten?

Please, Lord, calm our frenetic flights and landings, put an end to our persistent presence that drives all creatures to distraction, and give us a kinder death than those whose health we have taken away.

Amen.

The Prayer of the Flying Ant

Dear Lord,

Why is it that we termites are so hated, so eaten, so sought, when we are one of the most incredible little beings? Our exceptionally supportive and disciplined and complex social life, hundreds of thousands of us living in harmonised and caring proximity with our singular purpose of service to one another and our colony, to work unceasingly. We could teach so much to Your most beautiful of creatures, the great human race, with all their anger and greed and thoughtlessness, if they could but notice us.

When we were first born, hundreds of millions of years ago in the Cretaceous period, we were busy even then. Did we shape the earth with You, Lord, with our complexity of tunnelling and excavation? Are we Your best engineers, Lord, oh so busy in the darkness of Your good earth? Are they aware of their contamination and pollution, Lord, when all we are known for our brilliance are our antheaps?

*At one perfect moment with the midsummer
rains, the soldiers open pepperpot-sized holes and we,
the little nurtured princes and princesses emerge,
unfolding wings we never knew we had,
into Your light-filled, scented world above, Lord.
Ah, the incredible moment of flight, our four fragile wings
fluttering haphazardly, briefly, that moment of freedom,
never to return to the safety of our colony. Bittersweet,
terrifying, the workers behind us have closed the holes,
we falter in our wedding flight, our purpose to start new
colonies, and we hurry together, fearfully, mindlessly,
searching, searching. Oh Lord, protect us in the
moment of wingless search in the hot darkness of the
summer night. We are such feeble prey for Your hungry
frogs and lizards. So few of us survive. Oh Lord, protect us,
let us find our mate and our new home and frantically
dig its doorway! Oh, save us Lord, quickly!*

Amen.

The Prayer of the Frog

Dear Lord,

What a voice You have given us!

What power, what resonance. We can rend the night air with reverberation!

We can make ourselves heard many miles! For our size, that's pretty amazing!

Could they not just tolerate our seasonal croakings, our mating calls?

After all, Lord, we are pretty unobtrusive – just a part of Your wondrous creature portfolio. Can You hear us, Lord? CRRROAKK. Just testing.

Thank You for our jumping land legs. Thank You for our thrusting water legs. Thank You for our hopping abilities, our swimming speed and our adaptability to our surroundings.

Oh, save us from the snakes, the herons, those ever-foraging ducks! There are so many beady eyes upon us and our little wriggly tadpoles who have to fend for themselves.

*Although we are not much good at parenting,
we do give birth to such strings of eggs, filled with
faith in Your protection and preservation. We know
You'll look after them, and us.
We trust, we live for You, Lord.
We're fine, Lord.*

*Perhaps those polluting humans should trust a bit
like we do, Lord, and raise their voices in thanksgiving
and celebration like we do, Lord.*

Couldn't they look after Your world a bit better, Lord?

Can You hear us Lord?

CRROAKK!

Amen. CRROAKK!

The Prayer of the Glow-worm

I shine with Your light, oh Lord.
I shine for You – that tiny speck in the darkness,
a living, glowing light, for You, Lord.

I cannot dim it, for I need to show I am brave with
You watching over me, and I shine into the world
of darkness hoping, Lord, that my little bright presence
will make them stop in wonder.

But Lord, there is so little kindness and gentleness in the world.

Our tiny race is all but stamped out.

Instead of marvelling at the tiny glow I give, they
roughly pull me out of my sheltering space under the
leaves and in the rock crevices, and crush me and put
out my light carelessly, thoughtlessly, forever. Why Lord?

Once we were many, glowing so brilliantly in the dark,
we could light the way.

Now we are so few and we so rarely dare to glow for
fear of being crushed to death.

*We pray, we plead, for Your protection,
for it is for You, Lord, that we shine.
Are there any humans, Lord, who shine for You?*

Do they dare to glow or are their lights put out too?

Is there any hope, Lord?

Amen.

The Prayer of the Goat

Dear Lord,

*I am such a survivor! I am so agile, so undaunted,
so cheekily and everlastingly hungry!*

*Thank You for giving me so diverse a taste for things,
from the prickles of a thorn tree to the juiciness of melons,
from the grittiness of wayside weeds to the blandness of
washing on the line – it's all in the day's scavenging!
Such variety! Such inquisitiveness – such curiosity
You have given me.*

*See how I swagger around enjoying Your world,
Lord? Thanks, Lord!*

*I'm tough and brazen, I enjoy testing my bouncing
abilities on the rocks, and using those sure-footed
little hooves to scamper up the rocky hillsides in
search of more tasty titbits.*

*I don't ask for much, Lord. Your world of beauty
and bounty keeps me endlessly occupied.*

But I do fret during a drought, Lord – I become quite anxious. Perhaps it is because Your other creatures suffer so much – I feel their panic.

Remember, I am one of Your survivors!

Don't forget the rain, Lord! It makes Your world so beautiful, and so delicious! Thank You, Lord.

Amen.

The Prayer of the Goldfish

Oh Lord!
Those are the only two words we can mouth.

Oh Lord! But that is enough – we haven't much to say
except from our golden hearts to thank You, oh Lord, for
the preciousness of water and the cool roots of the water
plants and the welcoming shade and safety of the water lilies.

We silently glide and turn, unaware of the world in
crisis around our pond, and only become frantic when
our water heats up and dries and our life support is polluted
and stagnantly dimmed, and we flap helplessly.

Oh Lord! Protect us from the fish eagles and
kingfishers and the human polluters. Our life is so simple,
Lord, we ask so little.

May our brightness and beauty and our measured,
gentle movements instil in them some quiet, may they look
on us in calm and reflection, may we share our unhurried
serenity with them. Perhaps then, Lord, they will absorb
the wonder of our water world.

Oh Lord! Save us from the fish bowl, that terrible glassy orb that exposes us to distortions and captures us in fear and imminent death.

Protect us from fishermen and buckets and nets, from that ever-calculating cat on our pond side and give us clean expanses of water and a scattering of crumbs.

Oh Lord, hear our silent sounds.

Amen.

The Prayer of the Grasshopper

Dear Lord,

I am quite a handful, aren't I, Lord?

I have guts and arrogance and fearlessness, and those amazingly strong legs give me the edge, as I leap high and wide with no thought as to where I land!

I love outwitting and outplaying everyone! And I have the best of both worlds! I can jump and I can fly and I can crawl!

Thank You for my varied taste for anything that I land upon. I'll never starve, Lord. I love everything – flowers, grass, fruit, leaves, roots. I, and my tribe of relatives, those formidable and terrible armies of devouring locusts that can polish off a field in minutes!

I ask little of anyone, Lord, because I can outwit them.

I live in the moment, alert, yes, but lazily alert, on guard, yes, but unconcerned, watching, poised for flight, but relaxed.

*Some of my brothers exude a repugnant foam,
when in any way disturbed, some have sharp spines
on their legs with which they can draw blood.
An interesting band of vigilantes are we, but we swarm
only after the good rains, we are vigilant and
abundant in numbers and leave chaos
and wreckage in our wake.
Is it a shame, Lord?*

*Should I plead for Your abundant rains and delicious crops,
Lord, for my vengeful family?*

*All I ask You, Lord, is to keep me clever enough
to outwit, to outplay …*

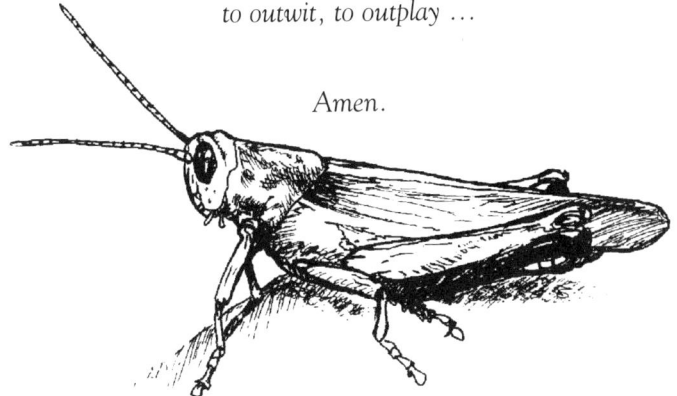

Amen.

The Prayer of the Guinea-fowl

*Let me speak Lord, my raucous voice grating
out my thanks for Your grass seeds and windswept
hillsides, on behalf of my brothers – we who love
flocking together – and
on behalf of the other heavy,
not-much-air-borne wild birds:*

*We live in the moment, Lord, scratching
and picking and loving Your seeds, Lord.
Seeds are our very existence.*

*We ask, with urgency, for a safe
place to rear our chicks.
Did You have to create so many foxes,
and jackals, and snakes, and wild cats, Lord?
They seem to spend most of their days
sniffing out our nests.*

*Our little race is dying out, Lord.
There are not many of us around.*

*Could there not be a 'Protection of Guinea-fowl Society'?
They make so many societies, Lord, what about us?*

We regret we offer not much in return,
but the occasional feather.
Have they ever seen such a feather, such shiny sleek spottiness?
Aren't we quaint, Lord? Big bodies, tiny heads?
They think we have no brains,
bird brains they call it.

How unkind, how rude, and how awful
that they have acquired a taste for stewed guinea-fowl.
And we're not really even palatable!
Lord, put a thought in their heads that we love dry
mealies, that we can be loved and tamed, and
would so enjoy walking on their lawns in safety
so they can enjoy our quaintness the way You do, Lord!

Amen.

The Prayer of the Hedgehog

Dear Lord,

*I am so little, so prickly, so flutteringly afraid.
So tentatively timid. So many of my family have died,
killed in such terrifying circumstances, those tar roads,
those fast cars, those bulldozers, those veld fires.
My little legs take such tiny strides,
I am forever fleeing, forever fearfilled,
forever forgotten, forever fainthearted.
So few of us are left.*

*No matter where I hide, they find
me and my tiny hoglets.
My prickly armour doesn't seem to work any more.*

*What is Your world coming to, Lord?
Do I not matter a scratch in the great scheme of things?*

*Am I here only to be hunted, crushed and
kicked like a prickly ball?*

*I have such a tender, tiny heart, I am so soft and
so warm inside, bursting love for You, dear Lord.
For I know You made my tiny feet in such perfection,
my beacon-guiding shiny nose with so exceptional a
sense of smell, my highly-tuned ears to catch every
minute breath of the faintest sound, so I strive to
exist for You Lord, I strive to cling onto
this fragile little life thread.
Let me live, Lord, protect my tiny life,
if only to show them the wonder of Your creation.*

Guide my tiny steps to safety, Lord.

Amen.

The Prayer of the Homing Pigeon

Heavenly Father,

You are the wind beneath our wings.

In that moment of ecstasy when our cage doors are opened and we can lift up and soar into the wild blue beyond, and whirl and wheel with the sun upon our backs in harmony and unison, we are consolingly closer to You.

For those first ecstatic moments of free flight and freedom, the wing-beat of our fragility knows no bounds. We are one.

You have instilled in us such incredible instincts and such a burning passion to return home. Do they know it too, Lord, our human handlers?

Do they feel Your compassion and ever-present presence there to guide each one of us home to the safe harbour away from life's icy winds and storms? Can they find their way too?

*Are they in awe, Lord, they who watch us,
their anxious upturned faces scanning the heavens
for our impossible return?*

*Are they filled with wonder that we, so small,
so fragile, light-as-air computerised missiles, can find
the tortuous route home?*

*Please, Lord, bestow on them gentle hands and
mercy as they take us further and further from home,
and quiet the terror in our little hearts that beat
to bursting in the returning.*

*Oh Lord, be with us as we search the vastness
for that unseen route, and guard and guide us
until we come home to You.*

Amen.

The Prayer of the Horse

Dear Lord,

Should You not have given me wings?
For then in my headlong gallop across Your fields,
I could take off and fly to You?

My body is so heavy, so big, and so trained,
captured, saddled and controlled.

Can they not feel the fluttering of my heart,
filled with such longing I could die?

They shut me in stables when I need the sun
and the starlight to grow and gallop.
They lead me with restraining bridles while I suffocate with fear.

They sit on my back and kick and spur my sides.
I try to do their bidding while I quiver with anxiety.
Can they not feel the ripple of my muscles wanting,
wishing, to be free to race, to flee, to fly …?

Thank You for the glory of Your meadows,
the lush grass and the energising air, but most of all,
Lord, help them to understand it is for You
I live while I serve them. It is
You I exalt in, with reverence,
for allowing me to experience Your world of wonder.

Oh, let me fly ...

Should You not have given me wings, Lord?
Oh, let me fly to you Lord.

Amen.

The Prayer of the Ladybird

Dear Lord,

*Thank You for my little brightness,
thank You for my little shell of spotted armour,
thank You for Your sun, Your flowers,
Your sweet dew and those juicy aphids.*

*Help me in my life-long battle to eradicate
them – they are such sap-suckers, Lord.
Why did You create them? Look at the damage
they do to Your precious plants!*

*But You have given me this satisfying task
of working for You, Lord. I am honoured to be
so large a part of nurturing nature,
part of Your great scheme.*

*I am the first really loved insect – is it because
I am so pretty in my scarlet and black
dotted designer outfit?*

*The children love me, Lord – but is my
tiny presence enough to teach them the laws of nature,
of naturally organic gardening and farming?*

*Make my tiny voice heard, Lord. I, like You,
am anxious that the world is not aware of the
importance of saving our environment naturally.
Am I a big enough presence, Lord?*

*Make them notice me, please Lord, before it is too late to say
Amen, Lord!*

The Prayer of the Lizard

*Thank You, Lord, for Your sun on the smooth
steps and the hot path. Cold-blooded and
scaly-skinned I relish warmth.*

It is here that I can patrol.

*I watch for those persistent flies, those follow-my-leader
ants, those whining mosquitoes.*

*I am vigilant, guarded, still, waiting.
Sleek and smooth, a solitary aristocrat.*

*I don't mess around, watching, waiting for my dinner,
I become a statue. Am I arrogant in my knowingness, Lord?*

I am unconcerned with others.

*I mind my own business – but
I am ever watchful, waiting …*

I ask little of life, a drop of dew, a few ants …

I am peaceful with just a little.

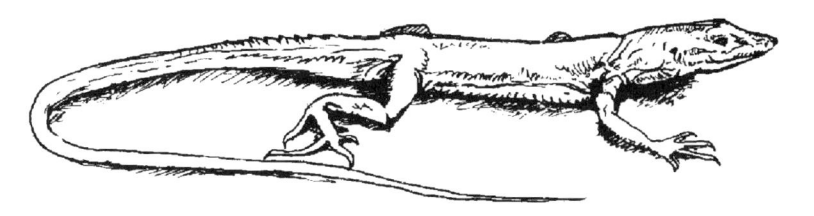

I am aware, Lord, that more is not better. Is there not a lesson there, Lord, for those whose greed desecrates our world?

I watch them scurrying to and fro, ever striving, rushing, getting.

I am still, guarded, waiting – but I see it all.

I watch, I wonder at all Your creatures, Lord.

Are You anxious too, Lord, at the pollution and contamination of Your world? Are You too watching and waiting?
Is there no end to the rush and the waste?
With the sleek swiftness and agility and alert quickness You have bestowed upon me, Lord, I can escape and elude those ever-searching predators – thank You that I can leave my tail behind when they do outwit me! It is utterly disconcerting!

But, Lord, I am observing, in my watching and waiting, that things are not as peaceful as they should be.
Let others learn to watch and wait like me – after all that is the only way they will come to know You, Lord, as I do.

Amen.

The Prayer of the Millipede

Dear Lord,
Why so many legs? Granted, it helps my
long body to move with a flow.
I glide with such a purpose and strength
and thrust, undaunted, hurrying to my destination,
which changes frequently – but hurry I must.
Disturbed, I roll into an excellent spiral perfection
in a single movement and I lie still and
unbreathing until they tire of my inertness.
That is my tiny protection,
unless a civet cat or a scorpion or sometimes
a timid hedgehog comes along,
then it is 'crunch' – and I am gone!

But I do have to say that my ringed armour does me
proud, Lord. It's a good deterrent and I can muster a
stinging sap that causes them to hastily drop me.

My plea to You, Lord, is to give me some direction.
My feet are killing me! All thousand or so of them!
The terrain is rough, we no sooner traverse it, than we silently
and silkily do a U-turn and we're off again, but whereto?

It is as though my feet have a mind of their own.
Perhaps one starts the rest off like a chain
reaction, next, next, next, next!

Let me thank You too, Lord, for the precious
rain and the moist and cool and friable soil.
That is what starts us off on our journey, heads down, and the
little waves of feet one after the other, up hill and down dale.
Just show me where we are all heading, Lord.
Is it towards You?
Then there's a purpose – thank You!

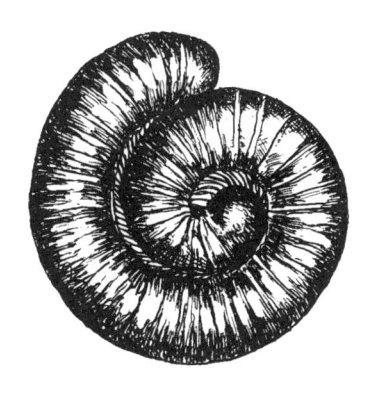

Amen.

The Prayer of the Mole

Dear Lord,

*Here in the depths of the earth and the darkness,
I dig, and dig, and dig.*

*Where I am going to, I am not often sure, Lord,
but I'll dig anyway.*

*I forge my way through the darkness of the sods,
making a way where there is no way, blindly burrowing
by inner purpose, strengthened by every exhausting pawfull
of Your rich earth that I silently push up, feeling my way
sightlessly into the outside world.*

Do they know, Lord, what great excavations I am capable of?

Have their tunnel-makers learned from me?

*Although I cannot be above in Your light, Lord, I can
still appreciate its warmth and the softness of the rain.*

*I can smell the rain, Lord, I can feel the sun,
I am safer here in the soft darkness than I am above.*

*I seek the moist meadows and soft banks of
Your life-giving soil, I make it fertile, I aerate it,
I enrich it for their crops.*

*Are they not aware that their harsh chemicals and
fumigants destroy Your soil, Lord?*

Are they blind, too, Lord?

*Can they not see that nature makes the only path that
we as creatures of Your earth can follow?*

*Oh Lord, save me from their proddings, and the burning,
smoking, poisonous exterminators – I am so busy
digging my way into Your paradise, let me live in my
silent activity for You, Lord.*

*I'm digging my way to You, Lord ... wait for me.
I am coming Lord.*

Amen.

The Prayer of the Monkey

Dear Lord,

What ability, agility and flexibility You have given me!

*I am the clown, with my gleeful acrobatics,
and I relish Your beautiful bounty!*

*Nothing defeats me, Lord. You have blessed me
with such low cunning, such perseverance and
such quickness of craftiness and daring that
I turn somersaults in delight!*

Thank You that I can scale Your trees in the blink of an eye.

*Thank You that I can fearlessly and raucously scold
those wretched dogs from my airy heights and
make a mockery of reason.*

Instil in me a little shame for my wanton waste, and messiness.

*Make me a little contrite that my adaptable palate is
insatiable and so excessively greedy.*

*Make me a little sad that I, tasting, tearing
and testing everything, get those stupid humans
to weep in despair and fury at the delectable destruction
I leave in my wake. Let me feel a little shame,
but not before I have stripped those ripening guavas,
oranges and pomegranates from their trees that
they planted just for me!*

I leap in joyful anticipation, just out of their reach!

Thank You, Lord, for so much – I'll always find it!

Amen.

The Prayer of the Mosquito

Dear Lord,

I am such a speck of wretchedness! Useless, hated, feared and slapped to death!

Is there no hope for me, the bloodsucker that I am?

I need the twilight and the night hours to search for those warm-blooded, breathing smooth-skinned creatures and I worry them into a frenzy while I feed thirstily, hungrily, my minute proboscis siphoning up my needed nourishment.

Couldn't they just stay still and calm and sleep while I hunt them down? Do they have to slap and kick and curse so frantically?

Is it I – so tiny, so pathetic – who can bring the mighty to their knees, robbing them of sleep, with my thin whining?

'Blood budgies', they call us in exasperation, 'mini vampires', but Lord, what is our purpose?

Are we not just disease carriers?
I and my multitude of brothers.
Breeding endlessly in shady watery spots?

Are we the lowest and meanest of Your creatures, Lord?

Are we merely existing to cause
a sore itchinessof red bites and bumps and malaria,
and, who knows what other contamination
we might spread?

Give us some hope, Lord,
or smite us away as they do, please Lord.

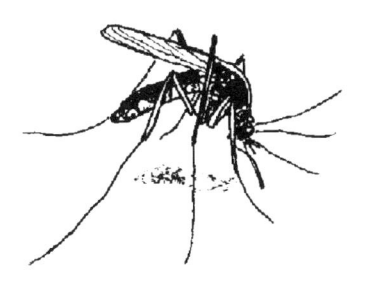

Amen.

The Prayer of the Mouse

How I scuttle, Lord, pounding of heart,
fleet of foot, permanently poised for flight!

How exhausting, Lord, how unendingly
terrifying is this fragile existence!

So many enemies, Lord!

Did there have to be so many?

Those sly, slithering snakes, Lord – how could
You have created them?

They silently seek, watching, waiting, in their dreadfulness.

And those devils with green eyes – always ready
to pounce – their twitching tails give them away.
But those claws, those sharp teeth and those silent paws,
those cats are deadly, Lord!

Take pity on me!

I'm not nearly as bad as my cousins,
those sinister, filthy rats, Lord.

What is their purpose in life, Lord?

*Perhaps I need to know more clearly
what my purpose is, Lord.
Am I really 'stinking vermin' too, Lord?*

Am I not endearingly little and all whiskery and agile?

*Can they not enjoy my cleverness instead of
standing shrieking on chairs?*

*I love to be near them, Lord, I ask only
for a few crumbs and a few seeds and a speck
of their delicious cheese!*

Why did You make me, Lord?

Please hurry and protect me! Quick!

Amen.

The Prayer of the Ox

Oh Lord!

What heaviness You have bestowed on me.
Heaviness of life – boring, unexciting, unstimulating.
What's it all about, Lord?

Once I was useful, I could pull the plough,
step by heavy thundering step,
I made a difference away from the tight confines of the kraal.
I could turn the rich earth in
searing heat and in biting cold, I plodded on
a field of dreams for their crops, their food, their lives.

So little is ever for me – restrained, chained and yoked.

My great mountain of meat is for their protein-sought
wellbeing. Dare I say their greed? They almost eat me alive.

The abattoirs are terrifying to our very souls, Lord.
Do You hear our appalling cries, our suffocating heartbeat?
Do You hear our anguish? Our terror?
The blood-filled slaughterhouse, Lord, is this what Hell is like?

*We, Your slow and heavy and unimaginative cattle,
castrated, prodded, tied and whipped, we stumble in pain.
Our only joy is a mouthful of Your sweet grass that we
thoughtfully, thankfully, chew over and over and over.*

*We longingly await our final journey to You, oh Lord.
But does it have to end in slaughter?*

Oh hear us, Lord. Why Lord?

Amen.

The Prayer of the Owl

The night is mine, Lord, thank You for the enveloping
darkness and the host of fascinating night-time activity
I am witness to. Unblinking, I watch. I am
the nightwatch – silent, sombre, solitary, I watch.

I am wise, Lord. I am truly the wise old owl
because I watch, and I think. A lot.
When in doubt – watch.
That's why I am so wise – I do not make
a hasty decision. I watch.

Thank You, Lord, for my penetrating eyesight – long-sighted
and wide-sighted, not even a cricket can move without
my seeing it. My silent approach on huge wings does not even
scare that wretched little mouse until I swoop for my supper.
Silent watching has a lot to be said for it, Lord.

My lonely heart-stopping 'Hoo-hoo-hoooo'
makes them morbid and fearful, Lord,
not only those restless humans, but it can also set
the dogs a-wailing and the rabbits a-flutter.
Could You tell them it's a song really?

*As I have no song to sing, I lift my strange hooting
into the night air, not to call their names, but to thank You,
Lord, for the trees, so hauntingly stark
against the night sky, that shelter me and my nest.
Perhaps they are unnerved because I watch
so silently from the leafy boughs.*

*Am I formidable, Lord? Formidable in my wingspan size
and solid strength and huge, unblinking, penetrating know-all
eyes? Perhaps I frighten them, but know, Lord,
I am grateful for Your caring and protection.*

I watch for You, Lord.

Amen.

The Prayer of the Parrot

*Am I not a wonder, Lord? With my colourful,
loud and raucous scratchy presence, am I not a show, Lord?
Of all Your creatures it is I, in my two-toed strut,
that can rivet attention. Soapbox style, I can spew out a
barrage of grating words that I mimic with measured glee.
If they but knew it, Lord, I am a sponge,
absorbing, storing sounds and words.*

I can shrill like the telephone.

I can ring like a bell.

I can bark like the poodle.

I can crow like the rooster, and it throws them!

'Hello darling, have a drink!'

*Can't they hear the
uselessness of their swearing
and their trite phrases?*

Would it not be better,
Lord, to have beautiful, kind and loving and
uplifting words as part of all our vocabularies?
Then they can spread peace and joy everywhere,
and I could loudly and persistently and continuously
repeat and repeat those precious words.
What a world we could have then, Lord.

I am content with my bowl of seeds, Lord,
and I love my mirror so I can seem to not be so
lonely when they go away and leave me caged,
confined and bored to terrible desperation.
Save me from that desperation, please.
All I ask, Lord, is to feel my wings. I need to spread
out the glory of those brilliantly coloured feathers.
Aren't cages made in Hell, Lord?
Teach them to be aware, Lord, to listen,
to be a sponge like me, and to speak only good words.
Words are the most important wands
that make or break. Let me speak Your words, Lord,
let me spread Your Love, let me drum it into them
and spread it into the world.

Amen.

The Prayer of the Peacock

*Our Father who art in heaven, who has made me
so utterly, so exquisitely beautiful, who has bestowed
on me feathers so scintillating, so vibrant, so lustrous
that it makes them gasp, how could You have
given me so shatteringly discordant a voice?*

*A voice that is so loud, so raucous, so gratingly terrible
in its strident cry, that it all but wakens the dead!*

How could You, Lord?

*It is not to say that I am ungrateful, no, Lord,
I am so beautiful, I love to parade, and strut my strut,
and fan my fan in front of their admiring eyes,
to show off Your brilliance in putting together those
breathtaking peacock blues and greens and golds.*

I bow before You, Lord.

What a creator You are, Lord!

*But, Lord, that voice! That tearing of the very air.
It sets everyone's teeth on edge!*

Perhaps, Lord, there is a lesson here.
Perhaps we should all learn to keep our
mouths – or beaks – shut. If we can't offer quiet
and pleasant sounds we should just shut it!

Is it enough, Lord, that I fan out all that beauty
in my tail feathers, and shimmer them for You?
Are You watching, Lord?

Forget the listening, are You watching, Lord?

Amen.

The Prayer of the Pig

Dear Lord,

Why me? Why am I so fat, Lord?
Is grunting and snuffling my only communication?
Why me, Lord? Am I Your only creature of ridicule?
Fat as a pig, dirty as a pig,
eating like a pig – even my pigsty is criticised.

I so relish the mud and the smells, Lord.
My snout is my antenna, I forage and scuffle about
on those ridiculously small feet,
ever-searching, ever-busy, ever-hungry.
Do I have to be so hungry, Lord?

Why me, Lord? Am I just the bacon and the ham
and the pork sausages and pork chops, Lord,
waiting for that most terrible day when my throat is cut
and I bleed to death like a pig?
Is my death drowned in blood?

My head is forever down, searching and foraging.
Is there anything above, Lord, that I could eat?
Is it worth looking up, Lord? One thing Lord
I do appreciate is the taste of all Your luscious fruits and
vegetables. I am essentially vegetarian, Lord.
Couldn't they be too? Couldn't they pig-out, Lord,
on all Your bounty? Wouldn't orchards and vegetable
gardens be infinitely more appealing than stinking pigsties?
Couldn't Christmas be roasted vegetables instead of me
and my friend, the turkey? Couldn't ham sandwiches
be replaced with cheese?

Why me, Lord?
Do I have to have such bulging fat roles and hefty thighs?
Oh save me from the pot, Lord,
and send me more luscious food troughs. I'm hungry, Lord!

Amen.

The Prayer of the Praying Mantis

Dear Lord,

*I am Your tiny prophet, Your little soothsayer,
I pray without ceasing.*

*I look deceptively meek, my front legs lifted in reverence
to You, Lord, but my fearlessness and strength far
outweighs my fragile frame.*

*I am the stalker, the watcher, the swing of my tiny head
on its flexible sinews which I cock so engagingly, endears me
to my prey, and they come closer as I sway sweetly to
lure them into my waiting arms.*

*Even I am constantly astonished at the lightning grabs my deadly
front legs perform to catch the unsuspecting moth or horsefly or
caterpillar, the quickness with which I devour the succulent body
and my neat discarding of the tough wings and legs.*

*Should I feel remorse, Lord? Or should I feel proud that
I am such a fearless and so impudent a little creature?*

Do they not see, Lord,
that I am encased in thanksgiving?
Do they not see how much a part of nature
I am in my varied and colour-filled dress?

Can they not realise how important I am in Your great food chain?

I keep the caterpillars, those greedy devourers, from destroying
the new leaves, I clean up the disease-carrying flies.

I have wings too, Lord, so I can fly to You and pray,
and my extraordinary egg-laying and hatching performance
should make them marvel at the wonder of Your creation.

I pray they let us be, Lord.

I pray that they too pray in gratitude and thanksgiving
for all the beauty You put before us.

Altogether now, lift Your hands in prayer, say thank You, Lord …

Amen.

The Prayer of the Rabbit

Dear Lord,

*Thank You for my light, swift, soft,
fleetness of foot – it is as though I am hardly pressing
upon Your warm earth – here one second and gone the next.*

*Thank You that I can outrace those snarling, terrifying predators.
Do there have to be so many?*

*Thank You for my marvellously sensitive whiskers,
my antennae that warn me so accurately of the continuous
approaching danger. Can they hear my thudding little
heart so filled with fear, with fright, with perpetual panic?*

*Oh Lord! It is so difficult to live with fear as
a daily, hourly companion.*

*My bright eyes and my speed save me,
and I bless Your grassy hillsides and protecting rocks
where I can crouch and hide. But Lord, does my
frightened heart have to beat so loudly?*

*Give me a tiny safe place to shelter my little nest
of babies, their adorable little bodies seek the
warmth and shelter of Your cupped hands.*

*We know You love us, Lord, but is it only at
Easter that others love us and think about us?
So briefly? Are we just a chocolate shape?*

*Oh! Quick, Lord! Hide me safely – here they come again!
I want to run to You Lord, show me the way quickly!*

Amen.

The Prayer of the Seagull

Dear Father,

I am one with the sea, the sky, the wind,
the salt spray. It is my home, my exaltation.
Thank You, Lord, for this sea space
You have given me. I need no more.
I am enveloped. I am content.

So few are content.

So few are unafraid.

So few are at peace.

So few can ride the storm as I do.

So few can lift up beyond the tearing wind and the
fog that clouds the way and darkens the day as I do.

So few take the time to stand and stare.

*They fight everything, resisting, struggling,
clutching frantically at wisps. Don't they know how
to just be, Lord? To trust, to accept, as You have shown me,
Lord, so clearly, so many times when I face the storm,
that in acceptance lies the overcoming.
Thank You, Lord, that I know how to let it happen
and to accept and to emerge triumphant.*

*I love Your beaches best, Lord, clear and clean and fresh
after the night tide, the debris gone and a new day ahead.
I leave my footprints in the sand as I check for washed up
crabs and fish. You provide so much, Lord. Bless You
for those silvery shoals of sardines!*

*I wheel and glide over the tides, watching the coming in
and the going out. I flow with it, I don't fight the winds
or the storms, I accept, knowing this too shall pass.
It always passes, Lord, and I soar up into the lonely sky,
echoing my lonely cry, with You, Lord, nearer and
closer, alone but unafraid for I know You watch over me.*

*Is there some way I can show them, Lord, how You provide?
How you protect?*

Amen.

The Prayer of the Sheep

Dear Father in heaven,

Of all Your creatures, am I not the most passive, the most accepting, the most silent, in my usefulness to them?

That I should be clothed in woolliness that they covet, that I should be succulently, flavoursomely fleshed, that I should blindly accept slaughter – I go like a lamb to slaughter, following closely behind my brother.

Is it not achingly sad, Lord? Am I just a living, breathing, brief profit for them, Lord?

They think there is only one thing more stupid than a sheep, and that is another sheep.

Is that not a solemn and disrespectful thought, Lord, when I give them so much?

Does it hurt You too?

Do they not have compassion for my little fragile lambs, Lord?

Do they not shudder at the lamb's killings?
Oh! It is too much to bear!

I give my wool, I give my flesh, silently, but hear my
lamb's wistful bleat, Lord, it is crying out for life!

Let me lie beside You, Lord, let me keep You warm,
let me comfort You, Lord, just a little.

You must be hurting too. That is all I ask.

Amen.

The Prayer of the Snail

Oh Lord,

It is my slippery slowness that defeats me. Measured, slimy, creeping, and oh so painfully, stupidly, slow.

It is this paper-thin lump of a shell on my back that hampers me – it is, after all, my home I suppose, but do I have to take it everywhere I go?

I look such a fright, Lord, all squidgy and soft and disgustingly slimy with my stupid little horns of periscope eyes on my silly little head, peering timidly into the world of light.

Oh, give me the darkness, and the moisture, then and there I am happy, and slowly appreciative of the shadows.

I crave a smooth path where I can glide on my silvery secretions, but protect me, Lord, from the night-time search parties with their torches and their crushing boots, and their ruthless hunting.

*I know I infuriate them with my devouring,
my insatiable hunger for their spinach and their lettuces,
and their soft and succulent plantings, but what else is
there to do, Lord, except creep into damp crevices in
the day and to prowl and devour relentlessly at night?*

*Am I part of the food chain, Lord – is that all I'm here for?
To be eaten? Sometimes by them, tit for tat, I suppose,
to get their own back, flavoured by the garlic I love
to eat in its soft young infancy.*

*Or, by those ever pecking, clucking, scratching hens,
Lord, and even worse, those screeching bantams.*

Hide me, Lord, slowly now, show me a damp nook, thank You!

Amen.

The Prayer of the Spider

Dear Father,

*I know that we are feared, but are we not extraordinary?
We are brave and free-ranging, capturing our prey often
many times our own size in those exquisite webs we weave.*

*Are we not incredible that we can travel so far on
that fragile silk thread by releasing it to the wind – by the
ballooning in the wind we can arrive at yet another
destination and anchor the thread there?
Aren't we brilliant? Aren't we the engineers
of the insect world creating silken dew-catching
webs that catch up our dinner so reliably?*

*All we ask, Lord, in our busyness, is for web protection,
our webs are our homes, our larders, and our life's work.
We fear the destruction, and their hatred of us.
Because they fear us, they try to exterminate us.*

*Aren't we, after all, part of Your portfolio, Lord?
Who has so many agile abilities, Lord?
Who can spin silken patterns of such ingenuity, Lord?
Who else has such diversity in form and in habit?*

*We offer the naturalist such a feast, Lord, from our
brothers those pretty, pretty, little pink or yellow or
green flower spiders, to the spitting spiders, to the sinister
violin spiders, to those clever trapdoor spiders, and on
and on – who else offers such fascination?*

*Couldn't they give us a break, Lord? We do, after all,
lure the flies and the mosquitoes into our webs.
Let us keep up that good work.*

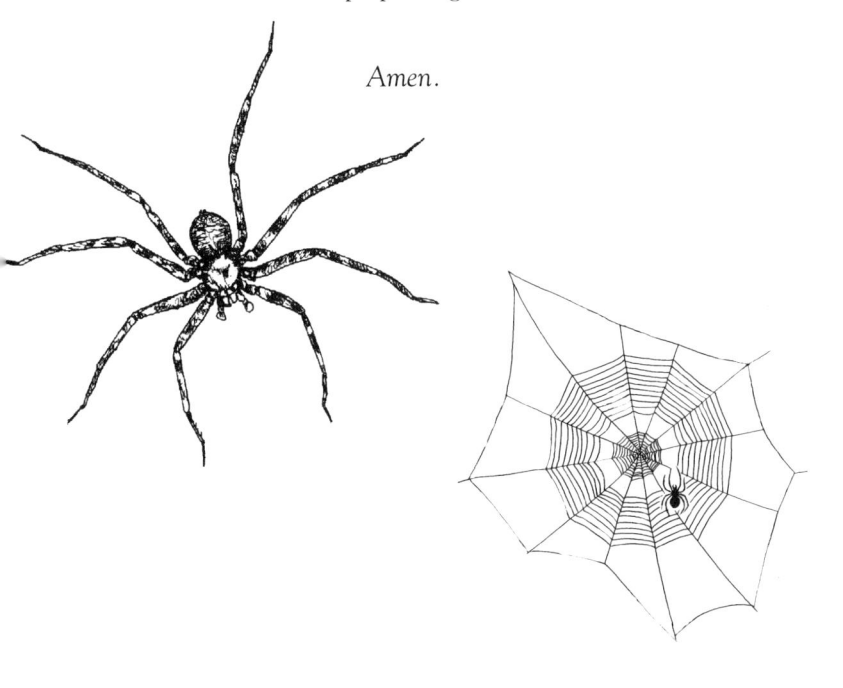

Amen.

The Prayer of the Squirrel

Dear Lord,

*I thank You daily for my quick-as-a-flash antics
and agility that enables me to outwit them all!
My smooth, scampering climbing abilities and all
this alert bright-eyed bushy-tailed exhilaration! Thank You!*

You have had such fun creating me – and I still live out that fun!

I am having a ball, dear Lord. Thank You!

*And I have mastered Your marula nuts – no other
creature can pick them out as clean as I can!*

*Thank You for creating such a bounty of food for me!
Perhaps I should leave more for others …*

*I really am nature's storekeeper! Make me just a little
bit more sympathetic towards Your other creatures who
are slow and laboured, especially humans.
I really do run circles round them!
But where is their joy, Lord?*

Or did You really give it all to me!

Sorry Lord, I must rush! No time to chatter with You, except to say in my dash that I am full of the joys of life!

Thank You for it all – and for Your oak trees!

Amen.

The Prayer of the Starfish

Dear Heavenly Father,

Have I not fallen from Your heaven?
Do I not belong up there with You?

I know I am one of Your stars, Lord, but I seem
to be so very far away from You.

Can You see me in Your pretty sea gardens?

I hide so carefully, Lord, because my bright star shape
intrigues them, and I dread the low tides when they fish
me out of my exposed rock pool, and hurl me relentlessly
upon the sharp rocks where I lie helpless.

Please, Lord, bring Your waves quickly to lap over me,
to return me to life, to my home beneath the sea.

Do these uncaring humans have to damage and interfere
with us so dreadfully? Destruction and stripping of the
rock pools and sea creatures is a daily occurrence.

Is it just for greed?

Is it just for fun?

Is it because they don't think or care?

Oh Lord! Save me from being washed up on those littered beaches.

Could they not be star throwers and throw me back into the embracing waves? They who trample and litter so effectively?

Could they not clean up the man-made debris and pollution that spoils the beauty of the shoreline and the seas?

Oh Lord, is it too late to save me – Your fallen star – and my sea home?

Take me up to Your heaven, Lord – it is safer there than here.

Amen.

The Prayer of the Swallow

Dear Lord,

Am I Your symbol of speed?
Am I Your living arrow? So swift, so sure,
so brave, so terribly, fearfully, anxiously restless.

Dear Lord, can I not be still, can I not find a moment
of respite, can You not let me find a breath of safety
and calm in the hollow of Your hand?

The summers call me too loudly and too often,
Lord. Your world spins so fast.
In haste I feel the urge to go, go, go!

No sooner have I braved that unthinkable migrating flight
across the continents and the oceans from Europe's autumn
into Africa's spring, then it's the wild calling to return.

Oh Lord, grant me the strength, let me feel Your loving hands holding me with my tender young fledglings as I guide them through the darkness, the icy winds, the storms, blindingly following my instinct to find, in the utter vastness of Your world, my nesting place, my little mud-packed home either here or there, with half a world between.

North or South, I fly over the Equator more reliably than those man-made aeroplanes. Am I not a wonder?

Oh, let them lift their eyes into Your heavens to watch my comings and goings and marvel, Lord.

Let them know the wonder of Your creation as I do, Lord.

Amen.

The Prayer of the Tortoise

I plod, Lord.

Heavy, cumbersome, my house going everywhere with me. I plod.

I am slow, slow-thinking and heavy in thought, heavy in spirit.

Slow – why do they all rush around and worry so? What's the hurry, Lord? Can they not stop and stare once in a while?

Can they not stop and smell the flowers, the intoxicating scents of the good earth after the rain?

Can they not appreciate the warmth of Your sun, Lord, the greenness of Your summer, the refreshment Your cool scent-laden breezes bring? What's with them, Lord?

Do they not know that the tortoise wins the race – slow, persistent, quiet plodding does the trick?

Must they rush around so fast, Lord?

*Do they not see the damage they do to their
hearts, their marvellous brains?*

*Should You not have instilled a little slow plodding in them,
Lord? They would be so much better for it, and the roses
would get smelled more often, Lord.*

*Thank You, Lord, that You have built me for safety.
Although I am heavy, I can defeat even the lion's blows
by just being still. Isn't that something, Lord?
Isn't there a lesson here?*

Amen.

The Prayer of the Very Little Bird

Dear Lord,

I am so little, so light, so terribly fragile,
born on the current of life.
I seek the shelter of Your cupped hands.
I fight against the wind, the storm, the winter, frost,
chilled to these tiny fragile bones, so terribly fragile.
Were it not for the warmth of Your sun,
and the nourishment of the dew of the morning
after the storm, I should blow away like one of
those dry ravaged leaves.
Thank You for another day where I can dart
with a quick clip of my wings into the wild blue above,
where I can sing praises of your divine creation
as though my tiny rejoicing heart would burst,
throbbing out my ecstatic song of praise.
Protect and guard my little nest, my little clutch of eggs
and my tiny, raw, just hatched babies.
Our lives are so wind-tossed, so terribly fragile.
Please Lord, bless the tree in which we shelter.
Bless the seeds and grasses and the flurry of little insects,
and most of all, thank You Lord, for giving us wings
so that we can fly closer to You.

Amen.